ublished by the
merican Association
f Colleges for Teacher Education
BTE Series: No. 6

Changing Teacher Education in a Large Urban University

CHANGING TEACHER EDUCATION IN A LARGE URBAN UNIVERSITY

by Frederic T. Giles

Dean of Education, University of Washington, Seattle

and Clifford D. Foster

Professor of Education, University of Washington, Seattle

for the AACTE

Committee on Performance-Based Teacher Education

July, 1972

American Association of Colleges for Teacher Education
One Dupont Circle
Washington, D. C. 20036

This paper was prepared pursuant to a contract with the United States
Office of Education, through the Texas Education Agency, Austin, Texas.
The opinions expressed herein should not be construed as representing
the opinions of the United States Government or the Texas Education
Agency.

Library of Congress Catalog Card Number: 72-81219

Standard Book Number: 910052-66-2

Preface

The American Association of Colleges for Teacher Education is pleased to publish this paper as one of a series sponsored by its Committee on Performance-Based Teacher Education. The series is designed to expand the knowledge base about issues, problems, and prospects regarding performance-based teacher education as identified in the first publication of the series on the state of the art.[1]

Whereas the latter is a declaration for which the Committee accepts full responsibility, publication of this paper (and the others in the PBTE Series) does not imply Association or Committee endorsement of the views expressed. It is believed, however, that the experience and expertise of these individual authors, as reflected in their writings, are such that their ideas are fruitful additions to the continuing dialogue concerning performance-based teacher education.

In this paper, the authors describe several performance-based programs at the University of Washington and the change strategies that were employed to convert former traditional programs to a performance base. The experience of this institution in changing teacher education provides useful guidelines to other institutions desiring to improve their teacher education programs.

AACTE acknowledges with appreciation the role of the Bureau of Educational Personnel Development of the U. S. Office of Education in the PBTE project. Its financial support as well as its professional stimulation are major contributions to the Committee's work. The Association acknowledges also the contribution of members of the Committee who served as readers of this paper and of members of the Project staff who assisted in its publication. Special recognition is due J. W. Maucker, chairman of the Committee, and David R. Krathwohl, member of the Committee, for their contributions to the development of the PBTE Series of papers.

Edward C. Pomeroy,
Executive Director, AACTE

Karl Massanari, Associate Director,
AACTE, and Director of AACTE's
Performance-Based Teacher Education
Project

---

[1] Elam, Stanley, "Performance-Based Teacher Education: What Is the State of the Art?." The American Association of Colleges for Teacher Education, December 1971.

Introductory Note

A major concern of everyone interested in PBTE is how it works in practice. The Committee was curious too, and visited a number of places which have developed PBTE programs. A part of our publication series is devoted to case studies of institutions selected on the basis of these visits. Further, a paper by Iris Elfenbein, which will be published shortly, pulls together certain general characteristics across a number of these programs.

Published as the second paper in the PBTE Series, the Caseel Burke description of the single-type program at Weber State College is the first of the case studies. Because this institution had no teacher education program in existence previously, it did not face the problem of converting a traditional program to a performance-base.

The two papers in this monograph constitute another of the case studies. The development of the parallel-type PBTE programs at the University of Washington involved the conversion of traditional programs to a performance base. The paper by Frederic Giles describes the enabling conditions necessary, as he views it, to bring about such a program. Although much of it may appear to be a statement of the conventional wisdom of administration, as a distillation of the experience of one who has brought into being such a program, it must be viewed as a selected set from the wide variety of conventional wisdom statements that could be made. Much of social sciences is like this, in that it serves to reenforce certain parts of the conventional wisdom of others rather than announcing startling new and unique findings.

The Clifford Foster part of the monograph describes the various programs at the University of Washington which, like all PBTE programs, are in a continuous process of change and are already somewhat different.

Hopefully, this and the other case studies will help the reader to sense what is realistically possible in PBTE at this time, so that he may judge for himself its strengths, weaknesses and overall value.

David R. Krathwohl, Member of the
PBTE Committee and chairman of its
Task Force on Commissioning Papers

CONTENTS

CHANGING TEACHER EDUCATION: AN ADMINISTRATIVE PERSPECTIVE

By Frederic T. Giles

Introduction

Can a large urban university innovate and change teacher education? The answer must be yes, since these institutions will be producing the majority of our teachers. These institutions are located in the midst of the cultural pressures which are demanding changes in education both in form and process. Large urban universities must provide leadership in innovation and change and be on the frontier of teacher education developments or the needs of school and society will not be met.

Unlike many critics, I do not find a shortage of ideas and concepts for change in teacher education. What I do find is the absence of an operational system sufficiently flexible and viable to promote, encourage, even demand, change so that those ideas may be put into effect. There is a *tradition* of inadequate resources for teacher education, particularly in universities where teacher education must compete with more exotic programs, which is now well recognized. I am, however, optimistic that a major overhaul of teacher education can be made if systematic consideration is given to the process of bringing about required changes.

This paper is an attempt to provide guidelines for changing teacher education, and to that end it is presented in expanded outline form.

Teacher Education in the State of Washington

The developments over the past decade in Washington have led naturally toward certification standards which--

- Place the primary focus of preparation upon performance.

- Insure preparation experiences that are individualized and organized in a rational and systematic fashion related to a professional role.

- Evaluate preparation experiences on the basis of competency standards.

- Extend the responsibility for professional preparation to include schools and organization of school paraprofessional personnel, most especially for intern and continuing career preparation.

- Insure an increased collaboration among colleges, schools districts, and professional associations in the intern and continuing phase of career preparation.

- Define the function of State standards as establishing categories of certification and providing the ground rules for determining the preparation experience.

Certification standards in the State of Washington encourage rather than inhibit innovation and changes. Many colleges have been developing prototype programs consistent with the best thinking in teacher education.

The State of Washington has made significant strides in--

- Adopting non-restrictive teacher certification standards.

- Developing collaborative efforts, including all agencies of education.

- Designing performance-based, field-oriented programs.

- Developing standards for evaluation of performance.

- Involving many people in developing teacher certification.

- Providing the working base for continual development and revision of teacher education.

- Taking a developmental leadership role rather than a restricting role in teacher education.

Goals and Objectives of Teacher Education at the University of Washington

Teacher education at the University of Washington has several fundamental purposes. These statements of purpose provide guidelines for the goals and objectives that undergird the operational program. Based on the assumption *that teacher education is an all-university responsibility*, the several programs offered by the

2

College of Education in undergraduate work are designed to accomplish several aims. They are designed to help the prospective teacher develop competence and sophistication in one or more teaching fields and to develop proficiency in the teaching process through study and practice. They seek to introduce students to the study of education as a basic social institution and to the profession of teaching. Through study, observation, and direct experience, they try to develop the understanding of growth and development in children, youths, and adults. They develop the understanding of teaching and learning processes as those affect the selection, organization, presentation, and evaluation of curriculum materials and resources for various age levels and ability groups. Lastly, each student is assisted to develop a workable philosophy of education and an appreciation of the ethical responsibilities of a professional educator in a free society.

Organizing for Change in Teacher Education

As a result of several self-study activities, teacher education at the University of Washington is undergoing serious attempts to change from what has been a simple closed system to an open one that provides a multi-track system leading to certification. Attempts to bring about change are occurring within the framework of an operational system designed to promote an improved teacher education program. The basic assumptions undergirding *the system for change* are essentially that--

● The basic factor holding back changes in teacher education was the lack of operational models for developing and carrying out changes rather than a shortage of ideas and concepts.

● Changes can best be carried out through a developmental process rather than through the testing of a research model or through a total conversion model.

● No attempt be made to change the entire program but that all efforts be directed toward developing alternate routes which students may select on a basis of past experience and/or future goals.

● All efforts must represent attempts to deal with production of masses of teachers without becoming mass production.

From these assumptions and as a result of planning activities certain *critical* program goals have emerged. In organizing for change, goals must lead to operational objectives which are implemented by activities that are evaluated in terms of objectives, accomplishment, and the results of the evaluation recycled in terms of revisions. This format can be used both in developing and evaluating the total program or any given goal and objective within the program.

For example:

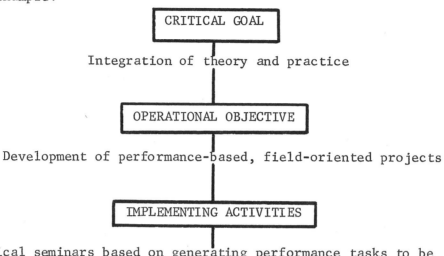

CRITICAL GOAL

Integration of theory and practice

OPERATIONAL OBJECTIVE

Development of performance-based, field-oriented projects

IMPLEMENTING ACTIVITIES

Clinical seminars based on generating performance tasks to be demonstrated in selected field settings

Special sections of courses correlated with field experiences

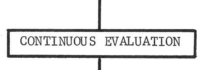

CONTINUOUS EVALUATION

Evaluation of relevancy of tasks and of scheduling concerns

Evaluations conducted through:
        Meetings and written evaluation of Clinical Professors
        Meetings and written evaluation of Field Coordinators
        Meetings and written evaluation of Field Associates
        Meetings and written evaluation of Interns

REVISIONS AND RECYCLING

Modification of scheduling of performance tasks designed to apply theory in field settings

Changed concept of timing between learning performance tasks and performing them

Changed performance tasks emphasis

GOALS	OPERATIONAL OBJECTIVES	IMPLEMENTING ACTIVITIES	CONTINUOUS EVALUATION	REVISIONS & RECYCLING
Integration of theory and practice	Development of performance-based, field-oriented projects			
"Block of time" projects requiring full-time commitment of students	Arrangement for teacher education courses correlated with field experiences in specified time modules sequenced over two or more quarters			
Recruitment of students representing a variety of ethnic groups	Development of projects designed to serve needs of various ethnic groups			
Preparation of teachers to work in selected ethnic settings	Development of experiences designed to prepare teachers to develop knowledge, attitudes, and skills related to selected ethnic settings			

-continued-

5

GOALS	OPERATIONAL OBJECTIVES	IMPLEMENTING ACTIVITIES	CONTINUOUS EVALUATION	REVISIONS & RECYCLING
Criterion measures for the evaluation of campus and field experiences to replace conventional grading system	Development of performance-based evaluation instruments (criterion-referenced and based on a conceptual model of teaching) for the evaluation of student teachers' and interns' field experiences			
	Provision for pass-fail grading in performance-based courses			
A coalition approach in the development, conduct, and evaluation of teacher education	Provision for the participation of field associates, principals, professional association representatives, interns, and University personnel in the development, conduct, and evaluation of teacher education projects			

-continued-

6

GOALS	OPERATIONAL OBJECTIVES	IMPLEMENTING ACTIVITIES	CONTINUOUS EVALUATION	REVISIONS & RECYCLING
Ongoing improvement of the quality of supervision of field experiences through inservice training activities	Development of extension-credit seminars for field associates in special teacher education projects			
	Development of bi-weekly workshops for field coordinators			
Conversion of the "supervisor" role to a "coordinator" concept in the field experiences program	Arrangements for the selection of qualified personnel to serve as field coordinators			
	Provisions for in-service training of field coordinators in performance-based instruction, conceptual models of teaching, and strategies of supervision			
Modification of faculty roles to accommodate conditions inherent in performance-based, field-oriented instruction	Arrange for the selection of faculty with commitment to the development and conduct of performance-based, field-oriented instruction			

-continued-

7

GOALS	OPERATIONAL OBJECTIVES	IMPLEMENTING ACTIVITIES	CONTINUOUS EVALUATION	REVISIONS & RECYCLING
Modification of faculty roles to accommodate conditions inherent in performance-based, field-oriented instruction	Arrange for reduction of teaching load to enhance assignments in special projects Arrange for selected faculty to develop close relationship with field personnel			
Screening of students based on a systematic admissions and selection procedure to include academic and personal criteria	Development of an administration system based on selection criteria peculiar to the various special teacher education projects and responsive to the teacher supply and demand conditions			
Controls on numbers entering teacher education geared to available collegiate human and physical resources	Establishment of intake quotas based on production models available for a given academic year			

-continued-

8

GOALS	OPERATIONAL OBJECTIVES	IMPLEMENTING ACTIVITIES	CONTINUOUS EVALUATION	REVISIONS & RECYCLING
Movement of students at varying rates of progress through the program according to individual mastery	Provisions for continuous progress of students as criterion mastery is satisfied			
Programs comprising interdisciplinary participation	Provisions for program planning by field committees including student and academic field representation			
Required experiences in community (non-school) settings	Provision for direct experiences on observation and participation levels in community activities			
Multi-track systems to accommodate students with diverse backgrounds	Development of projects designed for mature students			
	Development of projects designed for students with prior teaching experience			

-continued-

9

GOALS	OPERATIONAL OBJECTIVES	IMPLEMENTING ACTIVITIES	CONTINUOUS EVALUATION	REVISIONS & RECYCLING
Productive involvement of students in program development and evaluation	Development of media to provide student opportunities for involvement in program development and evaluation			
Continuous evaluation of teacher education to insure accountability and quality control	Establish evaluation procedures to include student, faculty, and field personnel participation			

10

Procedures for Changing Teacher Education

Changes in teacher education may go from a specific activity to a totally new program. Provisions need to be made so that any individual or group of individuals can propose and develop changes in the existing program. There must be developed a procedure for presenting, approving, and developing these ideas, as well as guidelines and characteristics of evaluating and considering them.

Every proposal should--

- Be consistent with and implement one or more of the goals of the teacher education program.

- Be conceived so that it can be implemented, evaluated, and finally adopted concurrently with other teacher education programs. This characteristic insures simultaneous accommodation of diversity in students and instructors.

- Be able to function within the state guidelines, available physical facilities, funds, and with existing or procurable field University personnel. This characteristic increases the possibility of an adequate trial period for every teacher education program.

- Contain at the outset--or by the end of an initial implementation period--a clear set of criteria for what constitutes a "successful" graduate of that particular program. This characteristic insures that every program can be, in fact, evaluated.

- Contain a detailed evaluation system which adequately determines the degree to which the foregoing criteria are being achieved. Included should be those who will conduct the evaluation, how it will be done, and when it will be done. This characteristic provides maximum assurance that evaluation will take place.

- Contain procedures for program modification or dissolution if suggested by the evaluation. This characteristic minimizes the possibility of any nonproductive program remaining in existence or going unmodified over a lengthy period.

Characteristics of a Performance-Based, Clinical, and Field-Oriented Teacher Education Program

Program development requires a frame of reference that provides definitions, conditions, and parameters necessary to facilitate communication and decision making. A document containing these provisions should be available to all participants in program development.

A Performance-Based Program Includes--

- Statements of goals for program.

- Performance objectives for implementation of program goals.

- Performance tasks for implementation of objectives.

- Criterion measures for evaluation of performance tasks.

- Provisions to insure a balance of theory and practice.

- Systematic evaluation to insure relevancy of assigned tasks for field and campus application.

- Inservice training to provide maximum effectiveness of campus and field associate teacher trainers.

- Ongoing evaluation of program to determine degree that program goals are being realized.

A Field-Oriented Program--

- Provides theory input in a campus setting with simultaneous or correlated field experiences.

- Relies largely on campus faculty to provide theory inputs and field personnel to provide supervision.

A Field-Centered Program--

- Provides theory input at the site where field experiences occur.

- Relies on campus faculty to give leadership to field personnel who provide theory inputs and supervision.

12

In practice, a program may begin with a field-oriented emphasis and shift to a field-centered base when a cadre of field associate teacher trainers becomes available in the field to provide theory input on site.

A Clinical Approach--

- Provides a system for the ongoing assessment of the trainees' strengths and weaknesses.

- Provides a setting where diagnosis and remediation occur.

- Provides alternate performance tasks for a given performance objective.

- Establishes a common, precise professional vocabulary to maximize diagnostic and remedial procedures on and off campus.

- Encourages continuous progress of the trainee at his own rate of development.

Policy and Decision-Making Processes Require--

- Cooperative development of the philosophy of the program.

- Adequate opportunities for campus (faculty and students) and field representatives to cooperate in program development, conduct, and evaluation.

- Continual dissemination of information to all participants.

Implications of Performance-Based, Field-Oriented Programs

When a college or university decides to develop performance-based, field-oriented programs they must be aware of the many implications for all persons and agencies involved. There will be a chain reaction for which all must be prepared. It is essential that each segment understand and accept these implications.

The institution will be required to--

- Promote teacher education and the concept of an all-institutional responsibility.

13

- Have an organizational structure which places the accountability for teacher education on the professional education faculty.

- Provide for meaningful involvements of all persons and units contributing to teacher education.

- Be committed to the permanence of a field-oriented program rather than a classroom-oriented program.

- Provide funds commensurate with the needs of a field-oriented program.

- Relate the resource needs of field-oriented teacher education to other professional type programs rather than to classroom type programs.

- Provide campus facilities which are oriented more towards clinics and learning centers than traditional classrooms but which complement rather than duplicate those in the field.

The administration will be required to--

- Pledge an inordinate amount of time, energy, commitment, openness, and, yes, faith.

- Believe in and use systematic planning and problem-solving procedures which use questions and concerns as fuel rather than barriers.

- Believe in the importance of teacher education as well as in the need for continual change.

- Believe that most meaningful change will come from those involved in teacher education.

- Believe that there is a need for operational systems that are flexible and malleable enough to promote and encourage change.

- See as an important role of administration making it possible for people with ideas to develop and try out these ideas within the goals of the college.

- Believe that one of the most productive systems for implementing change is a developmental process rather than the traditional research model or total conversion model.

- Believe that a major role of administration is running interference through or around rules, regulations, customs, and watch-dog organizations which prohibit or discourage change.

- Be concerned with accountability rather than control.

- Develop basic goals and objectives as guidelines for program development.

- Encourage and provide ways for teams of faculty to develop and implement ideas for change.

- Make decisions on the basis of what is good for implementing goals rather than on the case of administration.

The faculty will be required to--

- Assume a role as developer and coordinator of experience and activities leading to the role as teacher.

- Identify and organize the competencies, performance, skills, knowledges, and attitudes necessary for an outstanding teacher.

- Be involved at the campus as well as in the schools if theory and practice are to integrate.

- Work as a member of a team made up of persons from the various segments involved in the program.

- Select experiences needed by the student to become a teacher.

- Provide for individual differences of students.

- Provide sequential learning experiences so students can become independent learners rather than dependent learners.

The field will be required to--

- Demonstrate an interest and a commitment in teacher education.

- Develop and provide facilities for the program.

- Provide the time and dedication of personnel for the program.

- Believe in the value of involvement in teacher training.

- Arrange programs to accommodate the needs of the trainees.

- Believe in the benefits of teacher-trainers to the educational program of the district.

The student will be required to--

- Chose rather than drift into education.

- Chose from alternate paths to become certificated.

- Select a path commensurate with previous experience and/or plans for the future.

- Spend more time learning to become a teacher.

- Become a student of teaching.

- Become a more independent learner.

- See his training program as the first phase of a continuum of learning.

- Be judged on competency and performances.

- Become a part of the developmental team and provide feedback while in the program and after completing it.

Critical Factors for Success

- The willingness and ability to develop an operational process which encourages and stimulates a variety of persons from different backgrounds, different agencies, and organizations to work together to improve and change teacher education.

  The process must be open enough to provide opportunities for persons from the field and the University to ask questions, discuss concerns, discover alternate courses of action, yet provide direction and continuous movement.

- The interest and ability of persons, both in the field and the University, to assume changing and different roles from the ones assumed.

In addition, they must have the willingness and ability to
select and retain those persons who can play the new roles.
It also becomes essential that selection and continuous evaluations be made of the settings in the University, the school
buildings, and school classrooms which are used in the program to insure that they are good teacher-training places.

- The ability to acquire enough developmental resources to provide
  the flexibility and elbow room required for the development and
  change process.

  Teacher education has traditionally been geared to the classroom, the course, student credit hour, a professor, or some
  other such unit, so that time has not been built in for
  planning, new kinds of interrelated experiences, performance-
  based materials, continuous field experiences, and clinic
  and laboratory types of learning. These developmental
  resources need to be on a continuing basis rather than on a
  time basis so that the program can be in a continuous process
  of evaluation and change.

- The ability to acquire increased resources for operating a more
  personalized, performance-based, field-oriented program.

  Teacher education in universities and colleges has been considered a low-cost program by those who determine the different levels of program finance. It has been more closely
  related to classroom-type instruction than to clinic- and
  laboratory-type instruction. The resources required need to
  be objectively determined for the changed programs so that
  this information can be available whenever the programs are
  being considered.

- The ability to "retread" persons both in the school and in the
  University to carry out the developmental programs.

  Changes in teacher education are going to be carried out
  basically by people who are already in the colleges and
  schools. Those who have the interest, desire, and ability
  to perform the new roles will have to be identified and
  given opportunities and assistance to make the change. Care
  should be taken not to attempt to convert those who can't
  or won't operate well in the new roles. There must be
  alternate programs to fit the various styles of faculty,
  teachers, and students.

17

● The ability and willingness to establish enough satisfactory working relationships with other agencies in the field to provide adequate resources of training requirements.

Performance-based, field-oriented teacher education programs require close working relationships and willingness to work toward better teacher education rather than personal gain or convenience. In order to produce the number of teachers needed, the members of these so-called tri-partile arrangements will need to be numerous. Restrictions or interest in personal problems or power plays by the University, school districts, and professional organizations may render the whole idea unworkable except in special cases.

● The ability to create new and meaningful materials that put students into training units related to needs of the future rather than needs of the past.

Potential teachers should be in programs which exemplify the the type of learning situations which they are expected to provide as teachers. The experiences in which they are involved should be so developed that they provide for continuous growth by the individual as he or she becomes a practicing teacher.

● The ability to develop evaluation and assessment models consistent with the development process so as to better determine the payoff of actions taken to change teacher education.

These evaluations must be concerned with whether we are moving toward the goals and whether the changes made in the program are good, adequate, or better than other things which were done. Any assessment or evaluation must consider the development model which may not be in total development in the beginning but develops as a result of the process.

● The ability to develop specialized facilities that are essential for such a program.

The facilities must provide clinic laboratories and means for providing individual instruction and individual progress. The facilities should not duplicate those available in the field but should be a transition between ordinary classroom and the actual teaching facility in the field. They should provide for simulation projects and other types of activity which assist students to prepare for the actual experiences they will have in an actual school and classroom.

18

Administrative Problems and Pitfalls

Administrative leadership is essential if changes in teacher education are to be made and sustained. Administrators will require a firm commitment, a lot of enthusiasm, and boundless energy, as well as knowledge about the potential problems and pitfalls. The use of a problem-solving approach will be mandatory if pitfalls are to be avoided. The following are some problems and pitfalls which will be of concern to administrators as they move from a traditional low-cost program to the more complex, higher-cost program.

Instruction

A most important requirement is the changing of the instructional program in the institution from an accepted form to newer, less-accepted forms.

Problems that may be encountered --

- Changing the curriculum and instruction from traditional patterns to modules, self-instruction, mini-courses, simulation, and other techniques.

- Identifying and sequencing critical components of curriculum and instruction for teacher education.

- Providing for total change in instruction program.

- Developing a system for change which allows instrumental changes to be made and evolves eventually in total change.

- Developing a program that provides for the relating of theory to immediate practice.

- Creating an atmosphere for change in this field that will allow for and support newer directions in teacher education.

Pitfalls in administrative thinking to flag down: the idea that--

- Changing instruction from traditional patterns to newer patterns will come naturally and easily.

- A complete new package of instruction can be developed at one time.

- All segments of the instructional program will develop with the same ease or difficulty.

- Instructional theory can be translated immediately into practice in the regular school classroom.

Faculty

The key to the development of newer instruction and in carrying on the program will be the faculty.

Problems to consider are--

- The retooling of faculty in order for them to develop and carry out a conceptually different program.

- The acceptance by the professor of a different role in the teacher education program.

- The development of a proper mind-set by professors which will be as important as their ability.

- Getting professors to work more openly, cooperatively, in terms and in coordination with other segments of the teacher education program.

- Providing a conversion table for determining faculty loads so that courses, credit hours, etc., are not governing factors.

- Providing a compensating system for tenure, promotion, merit pay, etc., which is broad enough and flexible enough to include new roles and expectations for professors in the program.

- Providing a continuous system of in-service for the professors as well as the associates in the field.

- Providing the means for professors to spend adequate time in the field.

- Providing the means for releasing faculty to develop materials for new programs.

- Providing the means for classroom teachers to spend time on campus and in clinics with prospective teachers.

- Changing all members of the team to problem-solvers.

Pitfalls in administrative thinking in relation to the faculty--

- That faculty are prepared to move immediately into the conceptually new program.

- That all or most professors have the proper mind-set to develop and carry out the developing program.

- That all professors can work successfully in these programs.

- That constant attention is not necessary in order to protect professors involved in regard to tenure, promotion, salary, and faculty loads.

- That operational changes will take place without external motivation.

- That college administrators are not major factors in monitoring the factors which are important to the future of the professor.

Field Experiences

A most complicated part of the changes in teacher education deals with the use of the field in completely different ways than before. A limiting factor to changes may be the amount of the field which can be used in the newer training programs.

Problems will concern--

- Developing mutually acceptable perceptions of teacher education among professors, school administrators, teachers, and prospective teachers.

- Developing compatible perception of roles which professors, school administrators, teachers, and prospective teachers play in teacher education.

- Developing mutually acceptable ideas of critical teacher competencies among professors, school administrators, teachers, and prospective teachers.

- The scheduling of the schools and classroom which conflict with the learning sequences of the teachers in training.

21

- The day-to-day adjustments required in the classroom to accommodate teachers in training that are largely external to the basic educational program of the classroom.

- The necessity of teachers in training to learn to adapt to the expectations for regular teachers rather than functioning outside them.

- The development of a cooperative attitude and desire to provide conditions that will permit prospective teachers to function in a learning environment.

- The development of cooperating schools into more than field centers so they become lab settings for learning about teaching and not just apprenticeship centers.

- Providing adequate planning and developmental time for all members of the team from the University and the school.

- Providing a program for the classroom teacher who becomes a clinical associate for developing skills necessary to resolve the role conflicts between teaching and training teachers.

More pitfalls: thinking that--

- There is agreement on teacher education among the professors, school administrators, teachers and prospective teachers.

- There is agreement on the roles that each should play in teacher education programs.

- The schools and classrooms can and will schedule activities so teacher training fits easily into them.

- The insertion of teacher training into regular classrooms should not require unplanned and unforeseen day-to-day adjustments.

- Prospective teachers do not need to make frequent adjustments and adapt to basic expectations of the school.

- Prospective teachers do not need to be reassigned.

- All or most public school teachers can become trainers of teachers.

- All or most classrooms can become laboratory settings for teachers in training.

- The relationships between the University professor and field associates need not change.

CHANGING TEACHER EDUCATION: A PROGRAMMATIC PERSPECTIVE

By Clifford D. Foster

Introduction

The emphasis in this discussion is on the conceptual and management domains of program development in teacher education at the University of Washington in Seattle. In the preceding paper, Dean Frederic T. Giles has presented a frame of reference that is basic to gaining a realistic perspective of what follows in my presentation.

The concept of performance-based teacher education is firmly embedded in the design for program development at this institution. It has enabled the College of Education to make operational a substantial number of its goals that focus on the improvement of teacher education.

I have attempted to provide a baseline of information concerning program development since 1967. I have also attempted to provide an analysis based on the collective experiences of hundreds of individuals who have participated over the past four years.

Space limitations have not permitted a full accounting; however, I am hopeful that I have selected those aspects for discussion that will be interesting and useful to others who are engaged in program development.

Background

The concept of performance-based, field-oriented teacher education at the University of Washington had its beginnings in 1967 with the Northshore Project. This development represented a cooperative enterprise comprising a coalition of the University, Northshore School District No. 417, and the Northshore Education Association. Even though the project was a simplistic model, it has provided a prototype for most of the current special teacher education patterns at the University. It contributed the initial development and field-testing of baseline designs for the establishment of (1) a performance-based, field-oriented conceptual model, (2) a cadre of clinical professors, (3) a field coordinator approach for the coordination of field and campus experiences, (4) an inservice education program for field associate teachers, (5) a temporary certificate for teacher interns during the final phase of field experience, (6) an intern selection procedure including the participation of school district personnel in the screening process, and (7) a coalition management model based on a steering committee approach to decision-making related to program development, conduct, and evaluation.

Since 1967 several additional patterns have emerged and during the academic year 1971-72 it is anticipated that approximately 375 out of 1250 students completing certification requirements will participate in performance-based, field-oriented teacher education. The ratio of students in these special patterns to students in the standard program will have changed from one in fifty in 1967-68 to approximately one in three during 1971-72. This is especially noteworthy since all of the special patterns are on an elective base for students.

Students in the Standard Teacher Education Program complete course work in the typical traditional model. Theory courses and academic preparatory work are completed prior to one academic quarter of full-time student teaching. Further description of this program seems unnecessary since it closely resembles the traditional approach to teacher education that has been dominant in this nation for several decades. Here, as elsewhere, an atmosphere of discontent about the viability of this approach to teacher education prevails.

Impetus for changing the traditional program resulted from a report of the Dean's Task Force on "Teacher Education for the 1970's." The report, presented to the faculty Autumn Quarter, 1969, was prepared by faculty and student representatives. It contained recommendations for program development and included a system designed to facilitate change. These recommendations highlighted new directions reflected from numerous sources, including teacher education models developed under the auspices of the U. S. Office of Education; the proposed *Standards for Preparation of School Professional Personnel Leading to Certification,* Fourth Draft, State of Washington;[1] proposed *Standards for the Accreditation of Teacher Education* prepared by the Evaluative Criteria Study Committee of the American Association of Colleges for Teacher Education for the National Council for Accreditation of Teacher Education;[2] inputs from group hearings with student, faculty, field, and community representatives; and from observations of the Triple-T, Teacher Corps, EPDA (B-2) and related hard money projects sponsored by the University.

Subsequent program development efforts have been influenced by all these sources of input.

Rationale for Program Development

The following assumptions were formulated to provide a rationale for the development of new teacher education patterns.

1. That new patterns will be expected to include provisions that are characteristic of a professional program of study. These include an admissions program based on well-defined criteria, a predetermined enrollment geared to available collegiate human and physical resources, a specified block of time to which the student commits himself on a full-time basis, a multiple-track system to accommodate persons with diverse backgrounds and to provide for differentiated roles and conditions, a performance-based, field-oriented approach that provides for the integration of theory and practice, and a close working relationship between campus and field in the design, conduct, and evaluation of the enterprise.

2. That the principal agents or agencies participating in a teacher education pattern should have open access to decision-making opportunities.

3. That as new patterns develop, it is imperative that teacher education does not become transformed from one historically closed system to another new but equally closed system.

This rationale has generated seventeen critical goals for teacher education at the University of Washington. These goals are identified and described in Dean Frederic T. Giles' previous discussion. They will not be discussed here; however, selected operational consequences related to them that affect development, implementation, and evaluation are described in the sections to follow.

Program Development

At the beginning of the academic year 1969-70, eight developmental models were operational. These were separate projects, each designed to implement a specific approach in program development.

The scope of the special patterns for 1971-72 includes the continuation of four of the eight developmental models begun in 1969. Although the number of models has decreased from eight to four, the scope has actually enlarged when numbers of students and training personnel are considered. Three models were phased out as a result of discontinued funding on the federal level; one was modified to incorporate the participation of two additional school districts.

Students who participate in the special patterns normally are those who are in their final two years of the baccalaurate program and a smaller number who are post-graduates. Each of these special patterns is referred to as TEPFO (Teacher Education Pattern: Field Oriented) to differentiate them from the Standard Teacher Education Program. Thus over the past two years, a multi-track program of teacher education has become a reality.

Program Design for 1971-72

Analysis of program development over the past four years has resulted in a planning design based on a *conceptual* domain and a *management* domain.

Essentially, the conceptual domain incorporates the various aspects that deal with program components (e.g., rationale, program objectives, learning activities, and performance criteria). The management domain includes conditions essential to the planning, conduct, and evaluation of the various models (e.g., human and material resources and the design of the various decision-making models).

Implementation of the conceptual and management domains for the 1971-72 TEPFO models consists of three basic approaches.

Approach A

The development and field-testing of a training pattern based on learning modules, designed to prepare interns for elementary and secondary school teaching, is progressing in the inner city of Seattle. This approach provides for a training program scheduled across a preservice and an inservice phase with provision for continuous field experiences throughout.

Funding for the elementary level training program is provided by Teacher Corps and on the secondary level by an EPDA (B-2) training grant. Teacher Participants in the College's Triple-T Project serve as teacher trainers, trainers of teacher trainers, and also participate in the development of training materials for both programs.

The *conceptual model* for Approach A is based on clusters of learning experiences for interns and training personnel. Each cluster contains learning modules designed to provide the performance objectives, knowledge, learning activities, and evaluative criteria essential to its mastery.

The training program on the elementary level consists of five clusters scheduled over a two-year period. The first two clusters provided training experiences in a summer session prior to the opening of the public school term. One cluster was focused on the preparation of professional personnel (Team Leaders and Field Associate Teachers); the second was designed to provide preparatory experiences for the interns. For purposes of illustration, Cluster IA, "Preservice for Professional Personnel," contained eight modules. Three examples of these were contained in a module dealing with the philosophy and goals of Teacher Corps, another on performance-based teacher education, and a third on differential staffing. Clusters II through V are scheduled for completion by the interns throughout academic years 1971-73. Field experiences are provided in two portal schools. Since the preparation model utilizes learning modules, most of the instruction provided for interns is also done in the two field centers. The secondary level program is based on a similar conceptual frame; however, training experiences are scheduled over a single academic year.

The *management model* for Approach A is built around a steering committee with constituencies represented by the University, school district, professional association, interns, and community.

Approach B

The development of a systems design for a progression of teaching tasks in a continuous field experience over a two-year period characterizes this approach. Now in its third year, the pattern provides a paid internship for undergraduates in elementary and secondary teacher training. The University funds the operation and the Renton School District, located adjacent to the city of Seattle, provides stipends for the interns.

The *conceptual model* for this approach is built around ten general performance objectives. Training experiences, based on these objectives, are sequenced through a systems design that includes five primary areas: (1) the teacher, (2) the pupil and the learning process, (3) the structure of knowledge, (4) the instructional process, and (5) the environment. Each of these areas has one or more training systems designed to develop competency.

Systems Within Each Domain

The Teacher

1. Personal characteristics
2. Professional competencies

The Pupil and the Learning Process

1. Pupil characteristics
2. Learning process

The Structure of Knowledge

1. Structure of knowledge
2. Structure and concepts basic to each subject

The Instructional Process

1. Objectives
2. Diagnosis
3. Methods
4. Resources
5. Logistics
6. Evaluation
7. Sequence

The Environment

1. Society
2. District
3. Building
4. Classroom

Each system is being designed to include training protocols for sequencing the learning activities in accordance with the performance specifications described for the system. When completed, each protocol will provide for pre-assessment and individualization of performance tasks based on assessed needs. The design provides for recycling of feedback data for improvement of the system itself.

29

Following a September orientation, the training experiences are organized across two academic years, spanning an extensive phase of four academic quarters and an intensive phase consisting of the final two quarters. Beginning with the second quarter, interns are scheduled on a half-day basis in the field. During the final quarter, the field experience consists of a full-day assignment.

Inservice seminars are provided for the field associate teachers to acquaint them with the conceptual model and to provide opportunities for interaction of professional personnel from the campus and the field.

The *management model* for Approach B utilizes a steering committee similar in make-up to that described for Approach A.

Approach C

Since 1967, a major thrust has been directed toward the development and field-testing of a *conceptual model* based on a clinical approach to the preparation of teachers on the elementary and secondary levels. This is a cooperative, "hard money" enterprise embracing a partnership of the University and the Northshore, Seattle, and Shoreline School Districts.

The primary feature that differentiates this approach from the traditional arrangement of having a student teacher in the classroom for one quarter under the supervision of the classroom teacher is that TEPFO-Clinic provides a continuous field experience throughout the program. During this time, the intern develops competence in the teaching-learning process and strategies under the guidance of clinical professors, field associate teachers, and field coordinators. These professional personnel work together in classrooms and in a weekly inservice seminar to facilitate the conceptual model and to consider the problems of a partnership in teacher education. The intent is to immerse interns in teaching practices early, providing informational and conceptual inputs through the on-campus clinic and field experiences in the classrooms.

The clinical approach provides for the systematic diagnosis of intern teaching behaviors. Assessment of behaviors is done by clinical professors, field coordinators, and field associate teachers. Reinforcement and remedial protocols are scheduled in clinic and field settings.

TEPFO-Clinic: Elementary level attempts to reduce redundancy among certain aspects of methods courses. The on-campus clinic is organized around the themes of objectives, learner characteristics, development of criterion measures, prescription of learning experiences, and evaluation. Another important aspect of the on-campus clinic is the use of self-instructional packets by interns which allows for varying rates of progress.

Elementary level interns participate over three consecutive quarters. First quarter interns pursue language arts, reading, and art in the clinic in the afternoon and are in the field in the morning. They are involved the second quarter in science, mathematics, and social studies during the morning in the clinic and in the field practicum in the afternoon. During the third quarter, all interns are in the field full time, temporarily certificated under the direct supervision of field associate teachers and field coordinators.

TEPFO-Clinic: Secondary level includes a once-weekly clinical seminar on strategies of teaching and conceptual inputs designed to prepare the intern with baseline competencies organized around instructional objectives, learner characteristics, development of criterion measures, prescription of learner experiences, and evaluation. Interns also participate in a performance-based seminar in the evaluation of learning and a course in special methods of teaching, where required.

Secondary level interns participate over two consecutive quarters. During the first quarter, they follow a morning schedule in the cooperating schools. Campus seminars are scheduled during the afternoon. During the second quarter, the interns are scheduled in the schools full-time, temporarily certificated, under the direct supervision of field associate teachers and field coordinators.

The *management model* for TEPFO-Clinic: Elementary and Secondary levels is based on a steering committee arrangement that permits decision making by selected individuals representing the University, local school districts, local professional associations, community groups, and interns.

A Critique of Program Development Since 1967

Five components of program development will be analyzed in this section. These represent key programmatic areas contained

31

in the conceptual and management domains. Experience since 1967 has gradually produced a classification system that provides for the delineation of critical program development tasks. As additional experience in program development accumulates, it is very possible that modifications will be made in the classification system itself. Up to this point, the system has proven to be a useful structure for defining and sorting the numerous, sometimes minute, tasks that are essential to successful program development. The system also facilitates decision making since it reduces the possibility of confusing problems that are essentially of a management nature with those that are basically conceptual in origin.

Implementation of Programs

This aspect of program development falls mainly in the management domain. A coalition approach has been utilized from the outset in the establishment of the performance-based, field-oriented patterns. In each instance, the University has approached the school district(s) and local professional associations with an invitation to participate in a cooperative teacher education program. Following the approval of these two agencies, a steering committee has been established for the purpose of developing and monitoring the program.

The new guidelines for the preparation and certification of teachers in the state of Washington require that a *consortium* similar to the coalition described above be involved in the development of any new teacher education program that is submitted for approval after September 1971. These state guidelines are based on a process model for teacher preparation and certification. The model enables the local school district and professional association to have parity in the decision-making process with a college or university.

The University of Washington has pioneered an informal consortium approach, beginning in 1967. The new state guidelines stipulate formal procedures that must be followed for approval of programs by the State Board of Education. Consequently, efforts are now being made to formalize the process required in the state guidelines. Hopefully, four years of experience in cooperative program implementation should make the task easier.

Experience has demonstrated the importance of including field personnel in the initial stage of program development. Two critical programmatic provisions require early attention. The first of these, the definition of *roles and responsibilities*, is basic to the governance of the program. Shared decision making relative to the necessary role agents enables the planning group to allocate role responsibilities to the appropriate agency; i.e., the institution or the field. Early resolution prevents unnecessary confusion and conflict later on. The second provision is concerned with programmatic goals. Cooperative goal-setting by the institution and the field is vital to the smooth operation of the program. Early attention to this provision enhances communication among role agents and program participants and reinforces the concept of a partnership approach to teacher education.

Provisions for Program Management

The governance of the performance-based, field-oriented teacher education patterns is largely provided by the steering committees. This is management on the policy level. Operational decisions that are necessary for the resolution of problems that occur on a daily basis are made by designated role agents. Problems that cut across the interests of two or more agencies are referred to the steering committee if resolution cannot be achieved through individual negotiations. Final authority on decisions relative to the University rests with the dean of the College of Education. The assistant dean is the director of teacher education and, as such, serves as the coordinator for all TEPFO patterns.

The clarification of roles and responsibilities in a cooperative teacher education program requires much time and effort. Whenever there are personnel representing more than one agency, provisions must be made to prevent role conflicts as well as confusion of responsibilities. During 1970-71, task groups established by the steering committees described earlier in *Approach C* prepared a handbook containing role definitions and their related responsibilities. These handbooks have been made available to 1971-72 program participants. Examples of role agents and their primary responsibilities are:

Interns

> The success of TEPFO depends, to a large extent, on the intern's ability to assume a variety of roles and role responsibilities. Prior to the final academic quarter, the learner role is emphasized; the intern is a student of the teaching-learning process, functioning in a combined University-field setting. During the last quarter, although the intern role functions entirely in a field setting and shifts to a teacher emphasis, some aspects of the learner role continue, making it necessary for the intern to assume possible conflicting responsibilities simultaneously.

33

As a learner, the intern's prime concern is completing the University's requirements for certification and developing competencies considered essential to good teaching. As a teacher, the intern's major concern is the academic and personal welfare of his or her pupils in the field setting.

Clinical Professors

These individuals are members of the regular University teaching faculty who plan, conduct, and evaluate clinic and field performance tasks for interns. They are also responsible for providing remedial activities based on the diagnosis of weaknesses in teaching performance. These individuals are directly responsible to the faculty clinic coordinator.

Clinical Associates

This group constitutes University graduate students who assist with clinical and field activities.

Field Coordinators

These role agents serve in a liaison capacity, facilitating the integration of clinic and field activities. They frequently are ombudsmen in their efforts to establish positive communication among participants. They also assume the role of evaluator of performance by interns and field associate teachers. These individuals are local school district employees who are paid by the University. The role of field coordinator is extremely important to the success of a performance-based, field-oriented teacher education program.

Field Associate Teachers

This group comprises the largest number of professional participants. In some instances a single intern may be assigned to a team of field associate teachers. This practice usually occurs on the secondary level where an intern is assigned to a departmental chairman and a selected number of teachers within the department. The role essentially is that of a teacher; that is, a teacher of pupils assigned to him or her. As a teacher of teachers, he must assume a broad variety of sub-roles. He is a model in planning and implementation procedures, a critic, a counselor, a listener, and a morale builder. He also has the primary responsibility to evaluate the intern's performance on a daily basis.

University Faculty Consultants

In addition to the clinical professors, the University assigns
a faculty member to each preparatory pattern. The primary
responsibility of this role assignment is to provide consul-
tation to participants. The field coordinator reports directly
to the faculty consultant relative to the progress of the program.

Professional Association Representatives

A local professional association representative is assigned
to participate in each TEPFO field center. These individuals
participate in steering committee meetings and systematically
observe the program for purposes of informing and advising
the professional association.

School Building Principals

The role of the school building administrator is to facilitate the teacher education program through providing optimum
conditions within the school itself. He is also responsible
for designating interviewing teams to assist in the selection
of interns. He makes a vital contribution by encouraging his
faculty to invest time and effort in teacher education activities.

Specific responsibilities comprising performance tasks for
each role are provided in the TEPFO handbook. It also contains
selection criteria for each role. Already this effort to clarify
areas of role responsibilities has reduced the scope of management
problems encountered in the performance-based, field-oriented
teacher education patterns. Experience has proved that the iden-
tification of role agents and the delineation of their role responsibilities are two critical tasks in program management.

Provisions for Assessment of Performance

This area of program development operates on two levels of
the conceptual domain. The first level includes performance specifications for the interns and the second level provides performance
requirements for teacher trainers. Observational feedback has produced evidence that an inservice training program for field associate teachers is essential if intern performance behaviors are to
be assigned effectively and analyzed systematically. To this end,
continuing seminars are scheduled for field personnel who have

supervisory responsibilities. These seminars present information relative to program objectives and the roles and responsibilities of all participating personnel. Increased emphasis is being placed on the development of competencies required to evaluate teaching behaviors generated from criterion-referenced instruction in clinic settings.

The development of performance criteria was done originally by clinical professors according to the various curriculum areas to be taught. Increased emphasis is being given the development of performance criteria by field personnel and interns. Formative evaluation occurs almost daily. Summative evaluations are conducted twice-quarterly. At these two points, a performance-based evaluation instrument, developed by the director of field experience, is applied. This instrument is based on a conceptual model of teaching containing four domains of performance criteria. The model is an outgrowth of certain assumptions about the nature of teaching. A basic assumption underlying the model is that teaching involves behaviors that may be grouped under the (1) professional and personal, (2) instructional preparation, (3) instruction implementation, and (4) instructional evaluation domains. Each domain contains areas of performance behaviors. Categories of criterion behaviors are provided for each performance area. The evaluation instrument is used in all teacher education patterns, including the traditional standard program. In the TEPFO patterns special emphasis is given to the performance behaviors included in the instrument through instruction in clinic and field settings.[3]

There is much that remains to be done in the development of performance criteria. In TEPFO the product is evaluated according to the *performance* of specified teaching behaviors. This is far different from the traditional model where the product is evaluated by means of a letter grade based on academic achievement, personal characteristics, and the general attributes of planning, teaching, and evaluation skills. Interns are evaluated on a pass-fail basis for the clinical and field requirements.

The pass-fail determination is made on performance tasks required of the interns. All academic credits contained in the experience are evaluated in this fashion rather than by the traditional letter-grade designations.

The development of performance criteria presents a real challenge to clinical professors and field personnel. The problem has many facets, one of which is the necessity to provide differential criteria as opposed to a simplistic "go-no go" criterion for given performance tasks. Several possibilities are under consideration. One of these entails the provision for criterion

levels that would include a simple to complex continuum of knowledge and skills required for an intern to "criterion-out" on a
given task or set of tasks. Of even deeper significance is the
larger criterion problem that is concerned with the question of
what constitutes appropriate evidence to use in evaluating performance.

Provisions for the assessment of a wide range of performance
tasks in the field-settings has been a problem from the outset.
One source of the problem is the disagreement of clinical expectations for field experiences with the actual classroom schedules in
the elementary and secondary schools. This aspect of the problem
has been discussed on the steering committee level. Numerous
adaptations in performance task schedules have resulted from
cooperative clinic-field efforts. One of these adaptations has
produced a more realistic sequencing of intern tasks to be per-
formed in the field in order to conform with the sequencing of
the school day in the field classrooms.

In the final analysis, provisions for assessment of performance require a careful coordination of expectations that arise
from the various constituencies that are involved in the process,
not the least of which is the intern. Participation in the assessment of his own performance is assured for the TEPFO intern. The
graduate of this preparatory experience is expected to have demonstrated competence in self-evaluation. To accomplish this, numerous
training experiences, including self-assessment of videotapes of
his teaching, are provided.

Implications of Performance-Based, Field-Oriented Teacher Education

The previous section dealt with an analysis of selected
aspects of program development. In this section the focus will
be placed on implications of TEPFO for selected human and material
resources that are critical for its success. Space does not permit
a comprehensive presentation of these; hence, brief accounts will
be given of only those that have been persistent.

Implications for Faculty

Faculty who participate in performance-based, field-oriented
teacher education must concern themselves with management details.
For example, faculty responsibilities include frequent visits in

the field to translate performance criteria. Other qualifications
for faculty include the ability to work in teams with clinical
professors and associates, field coordinators, and field associate
teachers. Clinical instruction requires the capacity for faculty
to operate in an open, give-and-take setting with interns. Attention must be given to intern assignments that provide for varying
rates of progress. The style of instruction required in this
approach minimizes didactic teaching and maximizes inquiry and
problem-solving styles.

Efforts to solicit faculty participation have pointed up
the importance of modifying faculty loads to account for the
additional time and effort required in a clinical assignment. To
accomplish this condition, it has been necessary to decrease the
teaching load of clinical faculty by approximately one-third of
that required by professors in the standard program. The administration has come to recognize that, in the long run, faculty
promotional criteria need to be examined to guarantee recognition
for faculty participation in an assignment that demands increased
time for instruction and student contacts. Development of
instructional materials also figures heavily in this respect.

Faculty also have to be competent as trainers of teacher
trainers since the field coordinators and field associates are
expected to assume an increasing responsibility for instruction
as the program moves from a field-oriented to a field-centered base.

In general, faculty who participate in performance-based,
field-oriented instruction must have a strong conviction that the
initial preparatory program for teachers is a critical component
of the total teacher education program.

Implications for Students

Students who wish to participate as interns must so decide
early in their baccalaurate experience, in order to schedule
requirements in a block of time that precludes other academic
work during the interval. Prerequisites must be satisfied prior
to entry and this condition places a heavy responsibility on students and advisors.

They must also recognize that their success will be judged
on performance as opposed to strictly cognitive experiences.
They must also recognize that the block of credits acquired in
the experience are graded "pass-fail" rather than by the conventional grading system. Students exit from the pattern with
essentially the same grade point average with which they entered

it. This fact must be considered carefully by students who are concerned about elevating their grade point average during the final phase of their baccalaurate program.

Students are required to participate in many more activities than are required in the traditional pattern. Since the assignment requires continuous participation in a school setting, in addition to clinic activities, students discover that they are judged not only as students in the University setting, but also as teacher interns in a school environment. Thus, students are expected to acquire at an early stage many behaviors that are not required of students in the traditional program until they become first-year teachers.

Students must also recognize that they will be expected to develop the capacity for self-evaluation. This skill must be developed early and it also requires the additional competency of evaluating peer interns with objectivity.

Entry requirements include a screening interview in addition to the conventional entry requirements into the teacher education program. This fact sometimes performs a screening function in itself, since some students resist this personal confrontation and prefer the traditional program where no interview is required for entry. In most instances, however, students view the interview procedure favorably.

Students who elect the performance-based, field-oriented patterns must also recognize that they must forego many of the campus activities that would be available to them in the traditional pattern. Time commitments in the field preclude their participation in many campus activities.

Implications for Cooperating Schools

Responsibilities for cooperating schools are heavier than in the traditional pattern. School principals must exercise leadership in providing for those human and material resources required for the experience. Since students are scheduled over several quarters, problems arise that do not ordinarily appear in a single quarter of student teaching. The human resources that are required for a two- or three-quarter experience place heavy demands on a school faculty. Considerations must be made for the social and professional needs of an intern that affect others besides the field associate teachers. In many buildings physical resources must be strained in order to accommodate the social and professional needs of the intern. It is much easier to make these accommodations when a commitment for only one quarter is required. The extended experience requires a total faculty commitment; hence, care must be taken to assure that this condition is recognized and accepted by all.

Field associate teachers must be willing to accept additional responsibilities since they must assist in the translation and application of performance tasks and criteria that often require modifications in their curriculum for children. They must be willing to assign instructional responsibilities over to interns over a prolonged period of time. This requires additional management responsibilities. Field associate teachers must also be capable of working in teams that include the field coordinator and clinical professors. They must also agree to participate in the inservice, continuing seminars designed to enhance their participation. All of these demands require a dedicated professional who believes in the importance of quality preparation of teachers as a vital key to the improvement of the teaching profession. The professional rewards that accrue from participation are discussed in the following section.

Implications for Certification

Beginning in 1967, the temporary certification of interns in their final quarter was approved by the Office of the State Superintendent of Public Instruction. Since that time, patterns have been added that include intern experiences over a two-year period and, in these situations, temporary certification is awarded during the final two quarters.

In all cases, it is imperative that performance criteria be applied on a continuing basis to insure competencies of interns at the time when temporary certification is requested.

Experience has shown that temporary certification enhances the training experience. In the first place, it removes numerous problems of liability for all concerned. The intern is free to have the experience of "teaching on his own." This opportunity is very difficult to arrange in the traditional pattern because of the liability problems. The experience is also much more comprehensive because it enables assignment of increasingly complex performance tasks for the intern.

The provision for the temporary certification of interns also represents another enhancing aspect. It provides released time for field associate teachers to participate in various enrichment activities in the school district. It also enables the field associate teacher to differentiate instruction for children to a greater extent than is the case when there is only one teacher for one classroom. This adaptation begins early in the experience and is expanded markedly when the intern receives his temporary teaching certificate.

Temporary certification for interns provides the school with additional, sophisticated teaching assistance. To date, this feature has been received with general enthusiasm by interns, clinical faculty, and school district personnel.

Implications for the Provision of Essential Human and Physical Resources

This consideration can be reduced to the need for additional funding. This statement cannot stand alone as the total factor, since availability of funds does not necessarily satisfy the diversity of needs created by a performance-based, field-oriented approach to teacher education.

In the first analysis, funding does present a substantial variable. Since additional time is required for clinical professors to perform their assignments, slack must be taken up in those parts of the program displaced by their participation in the clinical assignment. This usually means reduction in the offerings in another part of the program or the availability of additional faculty as replacements. Additional funding is also required to provide the hardware and software needed in performance-based, field-oriented instruction.

On the other hand, the introduction of innovations in the total program necessitates revisions of all parts of the program to insure continuity and equity of opportunities for all students to receive a quality experience. Scheduling becomes more difficult in a multi-track system. Evaluation to date suggests the need to consider a block-of-time experience for the total program. This approach would require advance application on the part of the students. No longer would students be able to drift in and out of the program at their convenience. Efforts to assess the consequences of a block-of-time system are now underway. The concept of admissions based on *production models* already undergirds each special pattern. Intake of students in these patterns is based on the capacity of each training model to meet the demands of its operational objectives. The number of students in a model becomes a critical variable in this context. Availability of faculty and field resources are two additional variables that influence the number of students to be admitted. At this stage in program development, these problems present a serious challenge to the College for 1971-72.

The crux of the problem results from the fact that the College of Education is attempting to maintain a mass program of teacher education while at the same time making serious efforts to provide multi-track, performance-based, field-oriented patterns available to its students. Until sufficient baseline research data are available to demonstrate the superiority of these new approaches over the old, the College cannot completely abandon the traditional pattern. It must continue as an option until its credibility is destroyed. In the meantime, however, a reduction of numbers of students admitted to the program must occur. The College is currently exploring possible means to accomplish an overall reduction of students compatible with the number that each TEPFO Pattern and the residual Standard Program can produce on a quality basis.

The local school districts represent another source of need. It is vital that additional funding accrue to them for the realization of their responsibilities in teacher education. At this time, and in the foreseeable future, the University is unable to provide this funding. Other options will be explored. One possibility lies in state level funding to those school districts that participate in teacher education. Perhaps federal monies could be spent wisely in this way. These problems occupy a high priority for study in 1971-1972.

Implications for the Future

The past four years have produced evidence that performance-based, field-oriented patterns have met with a highly favorable reception. How long this atmosphere of favor will continue is a serious question. Program development in itself has many intrinsic rewards that accrue from participation in a new and exciting innovation. Additional funding to provide for the human and material resources demanded by sophisticated, expanding training experiences will probably be necessary to maintain that momentum in the years ahead.

A conceptual domain emphasizing performance-based, field-oriented instruction, and a management domain based on a coalition approach have so far proved to be viable organizational structures for program development.

Academic year 1971-1972 should provide the opportunity to refine the operational models resident in each domain and to

provide opportunities to establish research hypotheses that, hopefully, will provide objective data to permit continued change in
teacher education at the University of Washington.

APPENDIX

Assessment of Performance

The comprehensive performance of interns at the University of Washington is assessed according to criteria contained in the Performance-Based Evaluation Instrument. Prepared by Professor Norma M. Dimmitt and her staff, the instrument has been field-tested by University staff, field personnel, and interns. The field-testing process has resulted in several modifications in the instrument, and more are anticipated as additional feedback data are received.

This instrument is based on a conceptual model of teaching containing four domains of performance criteria. The model is an outgrowth of certain assumptions about the nature of teaching. An underlying assumption of the model is that teaching includes behaviors which may be grouped under four domains: (1) professional and personal, (2) instructional preparation, (3) instructional implementation, and (4) instructional evaluation.

These four domains are included in the evaluation instrument, with each subdivided according to performance categories and criteria. In Figure 1, the *Instructional Implementation Domain* is presented as an example of the relationship between the domains, categories, and performance criteria.

The evaluation instrument provides spaces for comments and checks relative to the degree of criterion mastery achieved by the intern. Used in this manner, the instrument constitutes a *summative* evaluation of the intern's performance at mid-quarter and end of quarter intervals. On these occasions, the cumulative evidence related to the intern's performance is reviewed. The summative evaluation process is comprehensive in that criteria related to each of the four performance domains are considered. The Instructional Implementation Domain contains three categories of teaching performance as shown in Figure 2. Each category is further subdivided according to criteria for evaluating performance. The user of the instrument is encouraged to supply additional criteria when appropriate. The asterisk (see Figure 1) in each category reminds the user of this possibility. The criteria are not intended to be applied exclusively; rather they are intended to provide the user with a performance-based frame of reference for the evaluation of teaching. Thus the instrument is essentially open-ended with respect to criteria.

Figure 1.

An Excerpt from the University of Washington
Performance-Based Evaluation Instrument:
the Instructional Implementation Domain

INSTRUCTIONAL IMPLEMENTATION

Manages Learning Environment
___enforces effective regulations in managing learning activities
___establishes workable approach(es) for controlling learner
   disruptions
___maintains a physical atmosphere which is conducive to learning
___organizes efficient use of instructional materials and equip-
   ment
*

Facilitates Instructional Objectives
___establishes motivation specific for learners and subject
___paces instruction flexibly, in terms of feedback from learner
   behavior
___modifies strategies and activities to facilitate learner
   achievement
___summarizes to reinforce learning and achieve closure
*

Promotes Instructional Interaction
___involves learners in active classroom participation
___stimulates learner questions, responses, and discussions
___promotes positive peer group interaction
___capitalizes on unexpected interaction and learning opportuni-
   ties
*

An evaluation resource guide has also been developed. It
contains selected examples of criterion measures for the performance criteria contained in the instrument. An excerpt from the
guide is presented in Figure 2.

Focus on a given criterion for a category of teaching performance; e.g., "Stimulates learner questions, responses, and
discussions" is sharpened through application of the criterion
measures suggested for it. Frequent *formative* evaluations based
on suggested criterion measures for a given criterion provide the
intern with objective feedback on his performance.

Figure 2.

An Example of Suggested Criterion Measures
for Performance Criteria Contained in the
Instructional Implementation Domain

Domain of Teaching Performance	Category of Teaching Performance	Criteria for Category of Teaching Performance	Criterion Measures for Teaching Performance Criteria
INSTRUCTIONAL IMPLEMENTATION	Promotes instructional interaction	Stimulates learner questions, responses, and discussions	Phrases questions to avoid misinterpretations and calling out of answers Invites and listens to learner questions and open exchange of ideas Elicits responses representative of convergent and divergent thinking Guides learners to methods of finding and testing solutions Avoids giving answers or repeating responses unless for deliberate focus *

Future application and testing of the instrument will be
required to establish the extent of its predictive validity. In
the meantime, assessment of performance as conceptualized in this
brief discussion has heuristic value for those who engage in it.

NOTES

[1] The proposed standards were approved by the State Board of Education, State of Washington, on July 9, 1971, and are described in "Guidelines and Standards for the Development and Approval of Programs of Preparation Leading to the Certification of School Professional Personnel," Olympia, Washington, 24 pp.

[2] The proposed standards were adopted by NCATE, January, 1970, and are described in *Standards for the Accreditation of Teacher Education*, National Council for Accreditation of Teacher Education, Washington, D. C., 1750 Pennsylvania Avenue, N.W., 22 pp.

[3] See Appendix for examples of assessment of performance based on the Performance-Based Evaluation Instrument.

The Texas Teacher Center Project

The AACTE Committee on Performance-Based Teacher Education serves as the national component of the Texas Teacher Center Project. This Project was initiated in July 1970, through a grant to the Texas Education Agency from the Bureau of Educational Personnel Development, USOE. The Project was initially funded under the Trainers of Teacher Trainers (TTT) Program and the national component was subcontracted by the Texas Education Agency to AACTE.

One of the original thrusts of the Texas Teacher Center Project was to conceptualize and field test performance-based teacher education programs in pilot situations and contribute to a state-wide effort to move teacher certification to a performance base. By the inclusion of the national component in the Project, the Texas Project made it possible for all efforts in the nation related to performance-based teacher education to gain national visibility. More important, it gave to the nation a central forum where continuous study and further clarification of the performance-based movement might take place.

While the Texas Teacher Center Project is of particular interest to AACTE's Performance-Based Teacher Education Committee, the services of the Committee are available, within its resources, to all states, colleges and universities, and groups concerned with the improvement of preparation programs for school personnel.

The American Association of Colleges for Teacher Education

The American Association of Colleges for Teacher Education is a national voluntary association of colleges and universities organized to improve the quality of instructional programs of teacher education. All types of four-year institutions for higher education are represented in the present membership. These include private and church-related liberal arts colleges, state teachers colleges, state colleges, state universities, private and church-related universities, and municipal universities. The teacher education programs offered by member institutions are varied. One theme dominates AACTE activities -- the dedication to ever-improving quality in the education of teachers.

AACTE carries out its program through the voluntary services of representatives from member institutions, a full-time professional staff at the Headquarters Office, and continuing commissions and ad hoc task forces. Projects and activities are developed to implement Association objectives. The Annual Meeting, held in February, considers current issues in teacher education and Association business as well as the development of acquaintances within the membership. Biennially, the AACTE sponsors a week-long School for Executives which provides an opportunity for concentrated professional attention to specific problems concerned with institutional teacher education programs. An important program of publications supplements the AACTE meetings and committee work. By means of the *Bulletin* the Association serves as a clearinghouse of information concerning the education of teachers. As a member of the Associated Organizations for Teacher Education, (AOTE), the AACTE works in a coordinated effort to improve the education of teachers. Through the Advisory Council of the AOTE, the cooperating groups are represented on the Board of Directors of the AACTE. A Consultative Service assists member institutions in working with specific teacher education problems.

The Association is a constituent member of the National Council for Accreditation of Teacher Education (NCATE) and as such provides valuable institutional backing for the Council's accrediting program. The AACTE provides important financial support for NCATE. Member institutions that are accredited do not pay a separate yearly accrediting fee, inasmuch as this is covered by the Association's yearly contribution to the NCATE.

PROPOSED FUTURE PUBLICATIONS IN THE PBTE SERIES

- A description and analysis of seventeen performance-based teacher education programs by Iris Elfenbein, Teachers College, Columbia University, New York.

- A scenario of how performance-based teacher education programs might look in the future by Asahel Woodruff, University of Utah.

- Problems in assessing teaching performance by Fred McDonald, Educational Testing Service.

- A look at the humanistic elements in performance-based teacher education programs by Paul Nash, University of California at Santa Barbara.

- The implications of broadening the base for decision making in teacher education by Michael Kirst, Stanford University.

- Two papers on the implications of operating performance-based teacher education programs in minority group settings: one by Joseph Durham, Howard University, and the other by Rupert Trujillo, New Mexico State University.

- Management of performance-based teacher education programs by Charles Johnson, University of Georgia.

- Alternative curricular designs for performance-based teacher education programs by Bruce Joyce, Teachers College, Columbia University.

The Series will be available for distribution in the near future. Communication should be addressed to Karl Massanari, director, AACTE PBTE Project, Suite #610, One Dupont Circle, Washington, D. C. 20036.

50

AACTE PERFORMANCE-BASED TEACHER EDUCATION PROJECT COMMITTEE

CHAIRMAN: *J. W. Maucker*, Assistant to the President for Academic Affairs, Academic Affairs Office, Kansas State Teachers College, Emporia, Kansas 66801

VICE-CHAIRMAN: *Donald J. McCarty*, Dean, College of Education, University of Wisconsin, Madison, Wisconsin 53706

William W. Barr, Student, School of Education, University of Denver, Denver, Colorado 80210

Elbert Brooks, Superintendent of Schools, Metropolitan Schools, 2601 Bransford Avenue, Nashville, Tennessee 37203

Patrick L. Daly, Social Studies Teacher, Edsel Ford High School, 20601 Rotunda Drive, Dearborn, Michigan 48123

K. Fred Daniel, Associate for Planning and Coordination, State Department of Education, Tallahassee, Florida 32304

William H. Drummond, Associate for Teacher Education, State Department of Public Instruction, Olympia, Washington 98501

Tommy Fulton, Art Teacher, Jarman Jr. High School, Midwest City, Oklahoma 73110

William A. Jenkins, Dean, College of Education, Portland State University, Portland, Oregon 97207

Lorrin Kennamer, Dean, College of Education, University of Texas at Austin, Austin, Texas 78712

David Krathwohl, Dean, College of Education, Syracuse University, Syracuse, New York 13210

Margaret Lindsey, Professor of Education, Teachers College, Columbia University, New York, New York 10027

Donald M. Medley, Professor of Education, School of Education, University of Virginia, Charlottesville, Virginia 22903

Youra Qualls, Head, Humanities Division, Tuskegee Institute, Tuskegee, Alabama 36088

Atilano Valencia, Associate Professor in Education and Assistant Dean in Mexican-American Research Program, University of Colorado, Boulder, Colorado 80302

Paul Varg, Professor of History, Michigan State University, East
     Lansing, Michigan 48823

LIAISON REPRESENTATIVES:

Theodore Andrews, Associate in Teacher Education, Division of Teacher
     Education and Certification, New York State Department of Education,
     Albany, New York 12204 (Multi-State Consortium)

Norman Dodl, Associate Professor, Department of Elementary Education,
     Florida State University, Tallahassee, Florida 32306 (Elementary
     Education Model Program Directors)

Harlan Ford, Assistant Commissioner of Education (or *Tom Ryan*) Texas
     Education Agency, Austin, Texas 78701

Norman Johnson, Chairman, Department of Education, North Carolina Central
     University, Durham, North Carolina 27707 (Southern Consortium)

Kyle Killough, Director, Texas Education Renewal Center, 6504 Tracor Lane,
     Austin, Texas 78721 (Texas Teacher Center Project)

Donald Orlosky, Professor of Education and Associate Director of Leader-
     ship Training Institute, University of South Florida, Tampa,
     Florida 33620 (Leadership Training Institute)

Benjamin Rosner, University Dean of Teacher Education, Office of Teacher
     Education, the City University of New York, 1411 Broadway (Room
     1119), New York, New York 10018 (Task Force '72 Committee on
     National Program Priorities in Teacher Education)

Allen Schmieder, Director, Program Thrust '72 Task Force, Bureau of
     Educational Personnel Development, U. S. Office of Education,
     Washington, D. C. 20202 (Office of Education)

Emmitt Smith, Vice President, Program Development and Resources, West
     Texas State University, Canyon, Texas 79015 (Texas Teacher Center
     Project)

STAFF:

Karl Massanari, Director
Albert Plouffe, Assistant Director
Shirley Bonneville, Program Assistant
Brenda Greenhowe, Secretary
Janice Chapman, Secretary

PUBLICATION ORDER FORM FOR PBTE PAPERS

Number of Copies	PBTE Series	
_____	#1	"Performance-Based Teacher Education: What Is the State of the Art?" by Stan Elam @ $2.00 per copy
_____	#2	"The Individualized, Competency-Based System of Teacher Education at Weber State College" by Caseel Burke @ $2.00 per copy
_____	#3	"Manchester Interview: Competency-Based Teacher Education/Certification" by Theodore Andrews @ $2.00 per copy
_____	#4	"A Critique of PBTE" by Harry S. Broudy @ $2.00 per copy
_____	#5	"Competency-Based Teacher Education: A Scenario" by James Cooper and Wilford Weber @ $2.00 per copy
_____	#6	"Changing Teacher Education in a Large Urban University" by Frederic T. Giles and Clifford Foster @ $3.00 per copy

BILLED ORDERS: Billed orders will be accepted only when made on official purchase orders of institutions, agencies or organizations. Shipping and handling charges will be added to billed orders. Payment must accompany all other orders. There are no minimum orders.

DISCOUNTS: A 10 percent discount is allowed on purchases of five or more publications of any one title. Also, a 10 percent discount is allowed on all orders by wholesale agencies.

Payment enclosed_____   Bill me _____   Amount _____
                               Purchase Order No. _____

NAME_____
                        (Please print or type)

ADDRESS_____

_____ZIP_____

Please address: Order Department, American Association of Colleges for Teacher Education, Suite #610, One Dupont Circle, Washington, D. C. 20036

ORDER FORM FOR RECENT AACTE PUBLICATIONS

Number of
Copies   Titles

            "The Profession, Politics, and Society" (1972 Yearbook)
_____   Volume I and Volume II @ $6.00
_____   Volume I (Proceedings) Only @ $4.00
_____   Volume II (Directory) Only @ $3.00

_____   "Power and Decision Making in Teacher Education" (1971 Yearbook)
            @ $6.00

_____   "What Kind of Environment Will Our Children Have?" @ $2.50

_____   "Social Change and Teacher Education" @ $2.50

_____   "Systems and Modeling: Self-Renewal Approaches to Teacher
            Education" @ $3.25

_____   "Excellence in Teacher Education" (Limited Supply) @ $1.00

_____   "Beyond the Upheaval" @ $1.00

_____   "In West Virginia, It Is Working" @ $2.00

_____   "Educational Personnel for the Urban Schools: What
            Differentiated Staffing Can Do" @ $2.00

BILLED ORDERS: Billed orders will be accepted only when made on official
purchase orders of institutions, agencies, or organizations. Shipping and
handling charges will be added to billed orders. Payment must accompany
all other orders. There are no minimum orders.
DISCOUNTS: A 10 percent discount is allowed on purchases of five or more
publications of any one title. Also, a 10 percent discount is allowed on
all orders by wholesale agencies.

Payment enclosed_____   Bill me_____   Amount_____
                                Purchase Order No. _____

NAME_____
                    (Please type or print)
ADDRESS_____

_____ZIP_____

Please address: Order Department, American Association of Colleges for
                 Teacher Education, Suite 610, One Dupont Circle,
                 Washington, D. C. 20036

55